Hold Me Close

Hold Me Close

Prayer-poems that celebrate married love

Ruth Harms Calkin

LIVING BOOKS
Tyndale House Publishers, Inc.
Wheaton, Illinois

Living Books is a registered trademark of Tyndale House Publishers, Inc.

ISBN 0-8423-3817-9

Printed in the United States of America

01	00	99	98	97	96
6	5	4	3	2	1

To Rollin
With all the love
Of my heart . . .

Thank you for showing me
So authentically
That love is a ten-letter word
Spelled c-o-m-m-i-t-m-e-n-t.

I love
Being married
To you!

Contents

Acknowledgments

The following poems first appeared in other Tyndale books:

"Confession," "Creative Conflict," "The Crown," "Futile Attempt," "High Cost of Living," "I Wonder," "Life's Detours," "Prayer for My Husband," "September Third," and "There Are Times" were previously published in *Lord, Could You Hurry a Little?* (1983).

"The Calendar," "Forty-Three Years," "Little Black Bugs" (formerly "A Better Way"), and "Right for Each Other" were previously published in *Lord, Don't You Love Me Anymore?* (1988).

"For Better, For Worse," "Future Mates," "Gift Exchange," "High Pedestal," "Hold Me Close," "Lessons in Patience," "A Man of Talents," and "Prayer for a Husband" were previously published in *Lord, I Just Keep Running in Circles* (1988).

"The Challenge," "Consolation," "Exclusively Ours," and "Unexpected Reply" were previously published in *Lord, I Keep Running Back to You* (1983).

"Birthday Dinner," "Cancelled Out," "Golden Anniversary," "He Said—She Said," "Help Them Just Now," "I Somehow Always Know," "Neat Arrangement," and "Other Husbands" were previously published in *Lord, You Love to Say Yes* (1985).

"A Better Way," "All the Way," "Are We Compatible?" "Baseball Season Again," "The Choice," "Creative Task," "The Dilemma," "Easier by Far," "Financial Status," "Forever," "A Gentle Memory," "The Gift," "God of Promises," "Healthy Change?" "Help, Lord!" "Hold Us Close," "I Love to Introduce You," "I Will Wait for You," "Living Realistically," "Marriage," "Never Too Late," "The Other Part of Me" (formerly "Discovery"), "Poignant Hurt," "Power

Status," "Prayer Request," "Rare Occasions," "The Reason Is Simple," "Remind Them Gently," "Squabbles," "Still More," "Suddenly We Knew," "Sunday Morning," "Thank You," "The Things You Never Do," "To My Husband," "Until Then," "Very First Quarrel," "We Learn So Much," "With Each Passing Anniversary," "Without a Single Word," "Words," "Wrong Choice," and "Your Glory, Lord" were previously published in *Marriage Is So Much More, Lord* (1979).

"Promise Kept," "The Quarrel," and "Wedding Anniversary" were previously published in *Tell Me Again, Lord, I Forget* (1986).

Finding Joy
in Our Love

It Still Happens

It still happens to me—
That flush of joy I feel
When my husband calls
Quite unexpectedly.

"Hi, honey . . .
Weekend traffic is heavy
So I may be thirty minutes late.
Will you wait for me?"
(I catch his smile over the phone.)

"Of course I'll wait
But I'd so much rather
Meet you halfway."

O dear Lord
You have been so good
To give us our love
For such a long, long time.

September Third

September third.
Our wedding anniversary.

Lord, I wonder why *today*
I should suddenly remember
One of our first ridiculous quarrels.
It wasn't at all funny then
But I smile now when I recall
My stubborn resentment—
My blatant retort:
"I wish you'd go fly a kite!"

In one shining moment, God
You seemed to pour all the love
From all the corners of the world
Into my husband's gentle voice:
"I will," he said disarmingly
"If you'll fly it with me."

We've been flying together
For thirty-eight years!

Morning Tribute

In all the years of my childhood
I doubt that we ever lived in a house
Where the sweet fragrance of roses
Didn't permeate the air.
I've never forgotten the summer ritual
That made every breakfast a special event.
Every morning my father would come in
From the backyard
With a freshly plucked rosebud—
His token of love for my mother.
Usually I'd be setting the table
When Dad made his presentation. . . .
"Here it is, sweetheart—
Your morning tribute."

One morning while sunbeams played
     leapfrog
On our kitchen wall
My mother stopped stirring oatmeal.
She dropped her wooden spoon
And threw her arms around my father.
I'll never forget her words:
"There are ten thousand ways of loving
And you know them all."
That's the story of
That's the glory of love.

I Dance and Dance!

When I'm all alone I dance and dance.
I dance all over our house.
I dance and laugh and twirl and sing.
I think I do it because David danced
In praise to the God of Creation.
With my total being I praise Him, too.
When my husband comes home
I still feel like dancing, but I stop.
How would I explain it if he said
"You didn't tell me you were into aerobics!"

Creative Conflict

I still remember
My Aunt Martha's saintly advice
The day before our wedding.
With genuine sincerity she said
"God will be living in your home
So of course you must never quarrel.
Just pray, and everything will be fine!"

But through the years
It hasn't worked quite so neatly—
With or without prayer!
Nobody is in control
Every hour of every day.
Emotional levels vary.
The important issue
Is not whether or not we quarrel
But how we resolve our angers.

Lord, thank You for teaching us
To handle our conflicts creatively.
So many things which disturbed us
In our early marriage
Seem inconsequential now.
Thank You for the sunlight of forgiveness—
For the liberating words "I'm sorry."
Thank You for reminding us
That learning to adjust
Takes years of mutual growth—
Growth stimulated by creative conflict.

Always Knowing

O dear God, how we
Thank You for each other—
Your incredible gift to us. . . .

The memories we cherish
The long quiet talks
The fresh concepts
The silent secrets
The cherished dreams
Starting over again
After please-forgive-me days.

So many beautiful hours
Of caring . . . or sharing.
So many God-taught lessons
So many newly discovered truths.
So many gentle hugs
So many pleading prayers
During days and nights
Of utter helplessness.

Shopping tours
Vacation trips
Summer picnics
Thanksgiving turkeys
Christmas tinsel
Family reunions

Anniversary dinners
Down-to-the-last-penny days.

Always knowing
Never doubting
Our love is here to stay.

Wedding Anniversary

Lord
Today is our wedding anniversary.
Thank You for the exquisite gift
Of love fulfilled.
You have made our marriage
What it was meant to be—
A dynamic demonstration
Of caring and sharing
Of giving and living.

When we invited You
To our wedding
That warm September day
(I still remember the blue blue sky)
Did You plan our joy then—
Or did You wait
Until You moved in with us?

Birthday Dinner

Here we are—just the two of us
Sitting across the table from each other
In this quaint old restaurant
With its nostalgic charm.
O Lord
When my husband called to say
He had planned a birthday celebration
I had no idea we'd be coming here.
How pleasant it is, how peaceful
To relax without feeling pressured
To chatter aimlessly, happily
To laugh at our own foolish jokes . . .

As we wait for our entree
In the flickering candle glow
My thoughts are ribboned with tenderness.
How is it possible, dear Lord
How is it possible
That we should still feel
This dear mysterious newness
After so many years of marriage?
But that's the way it is with You:
The best is always just beginning.

With Each Passing Anniversary

Please, dear Lord
Protect us against the subtle hazards
That so often threaten a marriage.
We'd like to think after thirty years
That we've battled through it all.
We'd like to think that it's time
To wave banners
And blow bugles
And shout to the world
"We've arrived!"
But the simple fact is—
Our marriage can be thrown into a tailspin
Anytime along the way
Unless we continually explore new heights
Pursue new goals
And deepen our spiritual concepts.
Lord, help us to make our promises
And renew our vows
With deeper assurance than ever before.
May we never be too preoccupied
To respond to each other
Or too selfish to cooperate
Or too indifferent to compromise.
With each passing anniversary
May this be our joyful declaration:
Never have I loved you
As much as I love you now.

Golden Anniversary

Just think, dear Lord
Today they are celebrating
Their golden wedding anniversary!
She is like a youthful bride
Still flushed with dreams
And he smiles at her
As though it were their wedding day.
In the reception line I asked:
"Does it seem like fifty years?"
Her blue eyes glistened
As she grabbed my hand.
"My dear, we're still just kids.
Think what God has waiting for us
When we're both with Him."

Right for Each Other

Thank You, dear God
That my husband and I
Are as right for each other
In the dull and daily routine
As we are in the quiet darkness.

Close Enough

What a flood of memories
Encircle the years
Since our romantic days of courtship.
How good to remember!
We smile, we even laugh aloud
When someone or something reminds us
Of the ridiculous moments
The stressful moments
Moments of planning and preparing.

I still picture one incident so vividly. . . .
We were sitting on a huge white rock
When you asked casually
"Honey, how much money do you think
I should have saved
Before we get married?"

A catch-breath
Almost a sigh—then finally
"Well, probably a thousand dollars
Would be enough."

Obvious concern
A glance skyward, then finally
"At this precise moment I have exactly
Thirty-seven dollars and twenty-four cents."

"Oh, honey! That's close enough!"

It's been close enough ever since!

Forty-Three Years

Forty-three years of marriage.
That's a lot of years!
Somewhere in a box of treasured things
I still have the postcard
I sent to my parents
While we were on our honeymoon.
I saved it because of its rare combination
Of humor and naivete:
"Bliss! Nothing but bliss!
Day after day of uninterrupted bliss!"
That sentimental bit of melodrama
Was written after we had given our marriage
The long, enduring test of—eleven days.
We had a lot to learn!

One thing is certain:
Whatever marriage was meant to be
It wasn't meant to be easy.
It's different when you're married.
You're accountable to each other.
You're making a life investment
In a permanent relationship.
At least that was our personal decision
Right from the very beginning.
True, sometimes I'm plodding
When I'd rather soar.
Or I'm submerged in soapsuds

When I'd rather be sunning on a sandy
    shore.
But when it comes right down to it
I wouldn't trade my lot
With any woman who ever lived. . . .

We lie side by side in the darkness.
Our fingers touch, our weary bodies relax.
Before we go to sleep my husband says
With beautiful gentleness
"I want you to know
I'm lying here loving you."

Forty-three years are a lot of years.
Lord, thank You for every one!

Are We Compatible?

We sit here quietly
In our peaceful living room
With a cup of fresh coffee.
I page through a current magazine.
I read, "Do you have a happy marriage?
Are you and your husband compatible?"

Well, I always thought so, darling
But let's see . . .
I'm always late; you're always early.
I'm noisy, demonstrative; you're often quiet.
I adore love songs; you prefer symphonies.
I go for details; you want the highlights.
I like to soak in the bathtub; you prefer a
    shower.
My closet is almost always organized.
Yours is almost always cluttered.

How disillusioning!
After all our married years
We suddenly discover we're incompatible.
But wait—let's not panic.
There's still the other side of the coin:
We love walking together in the drizzling
    rain
And hiking over hills on a crisp November
    day.
We love eating apples before an open hearth
And reading aloud to each other.

We love picnics and barbecues
And watermelon in July.

We love laughing and sharing
And singing and praying.
We love eating ice cream in bed
And whispering secrets in the darkness.
So—does it balance out, darling?
Shall we keep it going a little longer?
Are we compatible?

The Things You Never Do

Thank you for the things
You never do:
You never embarrass me
With crude, uncouth remarks.
You never criticize me
In the presence of others.
You never downgrade
My personal achievements.
You never compete with me.
You never compare me unfavorably
With other wives.
You never make me feel
Unnecessary or unneeded.
You never hide behind a newspaper
While we're eating together.
You never refuse to hear me out
In a controversial discussion.
You never remind me of past mistakes.
You never rule with an iron rod.
You never treat my parents unkindly.
You never degrade me.
You never betray me.
You never deluge me with
I-told-you-so's.
You never go to sleep
Without kissing me good-night.

Never Too Late

Her phone bill will be staggering!
We talked long-distance for over an hour
But how do you quiet love?
Excitedly she said
"I'm so in love.
He's everything I've ever wanted.
And oh, my dear
He treats me like a queen!"
Weaving in words between her delight
I finally managed to ask
"When will you be married?"
"A week from today," she exuded
"On my seventy-eighth birthday!"

How beautiful, Lord . . .
With You it's never too late.

Life's Detours

O dear Lord
With all my heart
I thank You for a husband
Who can enjoy the scenery
Even when we must take
So many winding detours
In our life's journey.

The Other Part of Me

You are the other part of me.
I am the other part of you.
I have loved you so deeply
For so long
But it will take
The rest of my life
To discover how much.

To My Husband

I sit on our comfortable couch
In the living room
Of our yellow house
A thousand miles from you.
I envision you
In the crowded hotel
In a lonely room
Lying on a narrow bed
Thinking of me . . .
And I know
Without the slightest doubt
That you are wishing
You were here
As much as I am wishing
I were there.
We were meant to be together
You and I!

Exclusively Ours

Through all the years of marriage
We've happily shared with others:
Our home, food, laughter, tears.
We've shared friendships and confidences
We've shared appreciation
We've shared music, books, flowers
We've shared victories and defeats.
But God, You've given us one priceless gift
That belongs exclusively to us
Not to be shared with another—
The beautiful gift of physical intimacy.
Thank You for its mystery
Its wonder, its delight.
May we never mishandle it.
May we respect and cherish it always.
May our self-giving continue to be
An expression of oneness
A celebration of wholeness.
Keep it alive, fulfilling,
And always full of surprises.
O God, what a marvelous expression
Of Your own fathomless love!

I Love Being Committed to You

This morning at the front door
Just as he was leaving for his office
My husband kissed me and said emphatically
"I love being committed to you."
I probably looked startled.
I don't remember that he's ever said it
Quite like that before.

Years ago, before God and to each other
We made a life commitment.
"As long as forever is"—that was our vow.
We didn't slide into it or drift into it.
There was nothing careless or casual about it.
We willingly assumed a personal
    responsibility.

Our commitment involves our investment
Of time and talent and energy.
It involves our moods and personal choices.
It involves our dreams and disappointments.
Our commitment tests our integrity.
It tests our ability to accept each other
Without debating, without reservation.
It frees us to explore, to climb
To keep our eyes on the goal.
All enticing detours lead to dead ends.

I've been thinking about it all day.
Tonight at the dinner table
I want to say it back to my husband:
"I love being committed to you."

All the Way

Somewhere I read, dear Lord
That You want us to have the most
Out of our physical intimacy—
Not the least . . .
That You want to bring
Into our sexual experience
An overwhelming spirit of sensitivity . . .
That You are eager for us
To celebrate our consuming love
In a pleasurable, exciting way . . .
That within our marriage relationship
You have ordained sex to be
An indescribable experience
A fantastic adventure
A rich fulfillment . . .
That You delight for us to share
Freely, generously, totally
In the most profound
Of all human relationships . . .
That You never intended our oneness
To be less than the best.
Lord, we're with You all the way!
Thank You!

Right Now

My dear husband
Right now
I am so content with you
So at peace with you
I want nothing
But this moment
Exactly as it is.

But why are
The distractions so many
And the moments so few?

Forever

Sometimes, my dear
I want to ask:
Why do you love me?
When did you first love me?
Are you sure you love me?
Do you ever not love me?
Do you love me more than yesterday?
Will you love me more tomorrow?
Will you love me a year from today?
Ten years from today?
Do you love me every morning?
Do you love me when you're asleep?
And then suddenly
All my questions seem foolish
And childishly immature.
I know that you love me
You know that I love you
And "love goes on forever."

The Reason Is Simple

I know it is true, my dear
That lovemaking is a privilege
And not a mere duty.
It is equally true
That in the intimacy of marriage
A sense of mutuality should exist.
But because of my love for you
And my honest desire to please you
Perhaps you are not surprised
When I tell you ever so gently
That there are those occasional times
When "duty" wins first place
With pleasure coming in as a runner-up.
The reason is simple:
You are the most important person
In all the world to me.

Other Husbands

So—other husbands
Come home late for dinner, too.
They rumple the paper
And leave shoes under the bed
And clutter the bathroom.
Other husbands gripe about budgets
And forget about birthdays
And steal the punch line
When you're telling a story.
Other husbands sulk like small boys
And refuse to admit they're wrong.
I made this amazing discovery today
While I lunched with four wives.
So no husband is perfect.
But thank You, dear Lord
That mine probably comes closest.

Neat Arrangement

He sat in our kitchen
Gulping freshly baked cookies—
Football helmet under his stool.
I asked, "How are your mom and dad?"
Quick response:
"Fine as ever."
Brief pause:
"They sure kiss and hug a lot."
Between bites:
"It's OK—we have fun together."
Eyes full of mischief:
"Husbands and wives are a neat
    arrangement."

Lord, thank You for Rick's parents.
Bless them for the love they demonstrate
For the atmosphere they create—
The goals they stretch toward.
Thank You for lovable Rick
With all his zest and enthusiasm.
Keep him steady and stable, Lord
Honest and clean
With his values held high.
Add maturity to his young conviction:
"Husbands and wives are a neat
    arrangement."

Someday, Lord, he'll kneel at the altar
(Frightened but elated)
With his own glowing bride.
On that day may he openly acknowledge
   You
As the One who wisely did the arranging.

Without a Single Word

So often you say *I love you*
Without a single word. . . .
When you reach for my hand
In the silent darkness
When you leave a love note
On the kitchen sink
When you empty the trash—
The task you most dislike
When you fold the laundry
Just to surprise me
When you make a special trip
For my favorite candy bar
When you awaken me in the morning
With a cup of steaming coffee
When you wink across the table
As we're entertaining guests
When you rub my aching shoulders
While I'm sitting at my desk
When you walk through the door
With a single long-stemmed rose
And a card that says
Just-Because Day . . .
When someone asks
"Does your husband say he loves you?"
My answer is always the same—
"At least a thousand times a day."

Baseball Season Again

One night on our honeymoon
I asked if you'd think of me
Every single minute
No matter where you were
Or what you were doing.
Do you remember, my love?

You laughed heartily.
Finally you said
"Do you mind if occasionally
I wonder who's winning
The World Series?"

That was years ago.
It's baseball season again.
And no . . .
I don't mind!

I Love to Introduce You

I love to introduce you
As my husband in a mingling crowd.
I love your firm handclasp
Your smiling eyes, your genuine laugh.
I'm proud to stand by your side
When you say with honest enthusiasm
"It's a pleasure to meet you!"
I like the way you put guests at ease
The way you center in on them.
I like the questions you ask—
Pertinent and direct—
To show your interest and concern.
I never feel stranded when we're together.
You are never neglectful.
I never have to turn to someone else
For response or support.
You make me feel confident and content
And always very sure of your love.
I look at other couples.
I listen, I smile, I share
But my heart always turns toward you.
Even in a crowd
The longer we're together
The more I learn of love.

Thank You

Thank you . . .
For thoughtful conversations
That stimulate my thinking
And clarify my muddy concepts.

Thank you . . .
For setting off chords of laughter
At unexpected moments
And for helping me see
That life is not always as serious
As I am determined to make it.

Thank you . . .
For listening with your heart
And for proving again and again
That love is something you do.

Thank you . . .
For your faith in my potential
And for your deep assurance
That God is eager to use me now.

Thank you . . .
For the stability you give
The encouragement you pour out
The surprises you plan
The fears you destroy.

Thank you . . .
For being an authentic example
Of my firm, forceful conviction
That love is a ten-letter word
Spelled c-o-m-m-i-t-m-e-n-t.

Thank you . . .
For being my husband!

Third of the Month

My husband woke me up this morning with
"Happy third-of-the-month, honey!"
Not a single time in our years of marriage
Have we missed celebrating our
    anniversary
On the third of each month.

Not big things, not expensive gifts
Certainly not a dozen red roses.
Just small remembrances:
A short love note, maybe
Or a favorite candy bar.
Sometimes a "festive" evening out
For a hamburger and a Coke.
Crazy little things, unplanned things.

It's been wonderful!
Neither of us can imagine
Not celebrating each third-of-the-month.
It keeps the spice in our marriage.
It keeps us aware
That love is something you do.
It keeps memories alive.

It does another beneficial thing
Which we notice with the passing years.
We may forget names and phone numbers
We may forget to put gas in our car
But we're both very confident
We'll never forget September third—
Our wedding day so many years ago.

We Learn So Much

I know I sometimes hurt you . . .
And sometimes you hurt me, too.
We have great days—deliciously great!
On those days we affirm each other
We listen, we share, we laugh.
But once in a while we have a lousy day—
About as lousy as a day can get.
On the lousy days we exhibit
All kinds of defensive attitudes.
We wave flags of rebellion
And hurl our painful platitudes.
We get picky, petty, rigid, harsh.
We feel threatened, rejected.
We blast our way through.
On the lousy days
Nobody would dare suggest
We're simply projecting
Our own shelved tendencies.
But, darling—
With all our whirling emotions
Tumbling together like laundry
In an automatic washer
We still know deep within
That our love grows more solid
With each added year.
We know that *forgiveness*
Is the one thing
That draws out the poison
And makes us whole again.

We know that today's heartache
Is so often tomorrow's nostalgia.

So thank you, my love
For so many great days.
Thank you, too, for the lousy days.
We learn so much in the mix!

You Are My Poem

Such a wild day
Going, coming, always running
Telephone and doorbell jangling
Nothing finished, nothing gained
I feel so utterly depleted.
Has anything I've done today
Been at all worthwhile?

Tonight as I was frantically typing
My husband left his favorite chair
Wrapped his arms around me
And said, "Are you writing a new poem?
Please read it to me when you finish—
Maybe I'll be in it."
Absorbed in his warm, gentle love
Suddenly my rapid pace stilled.
Dearest one, you are my poem.
No more typing tonight.

Walking with
God, Together

Hold Me Close

A little while ago
I said to my husband
"You're very quiet tonight—
You've spoken only a few words.
Is everything all right?"
"Everything is fine," he said.
"I really don't think
We need a lot of words.
I just want to hold you close."

Lord, sometimes
When You seem so silent
Is it that way with You?
Do You just want to hold me close?
If so, forgive me
For flinging my whys
And begging for explanations.
Forgive me for complaining about delays.
Help me just to quietly rest
In the shelter of Your arms
While You hold me close.

The Great Discovery

Years ago we discovered
That we simply
Could not be God to each other.
It is utterly impossible
For any couple to find in each other
What can be found in God alone.
How insecure we would be
If our dependency
Centered on anyone or anything
That we could lose.
But God is our security—
God, who can never be lost.
In every marriage it is always
The greater commitment to God
That makes the lesser commitment
To each other
As shining as silver
And as durable as gold.

There Are Times

There are times when we disagree—
My husband and I.
There are times when we frustrate each
    other
And say cutting things—
So cutting that we're filled with remorse.
There are times when we criticize and
    analyze—
Times when we must hold each other tight
And ask each other's forgiveness.
But in all our years of marriage
Never are there times
When we don't love each other
With genuine, gigantic love.
Thank You, God
Oh, thank You for that!

Help, Lord!

On our beautiful sunlit wedding day
I said "I do" with all the devotion
Of my ecstatic heart.
If I had known that day
All that I know now
I would have said "I do"
Just as eagerly, just as joyfully.
But I would have added
One quick secret plea:
"Help, Lord!"

A Gentle Memory

A gentle memory tugs at my heart—
The memory of a long-ago August night
When we sat at the round oak table
Addressing wedding invitations.
The list was long, darling
And our fingers curled.
As we put the last stamp
On the last beige envelope
You said with a challenging smile
"The first miracle Jesus performed
Was at the wedding in Cana.
Why don't we invite Him to *our* wedding
Before we invite anyone else!"
So we moved, just the two of us
To the dimly lit living room
And asked Jesus Christ
To give us the joy of His presence
On our happy wedding day.
Then we invited Him to live with us
In our home, in our lives, forever.
Of course He said, "Yes!"
He's been living with us ever since.

We Will Certainly Make It

No, my darling
We are not going to have a perfect marriage.
No, we shall not experience
Only sweet and tender happiness.
We will not adore each other
Let alone like each other every moment of
    the day.
We will not cherish and obey
In sickness and health
For richer or poorer day after day after day.

Nor shall we have peace and contentment
Undivided attention
Acceptance and forgiveness
Without a single interruption
As long as we both shall live.

But yes, we will certainly make it!
It will be a beautiful adventure
As we experience our own limited resources
And God's limitless power.
He will teach us how to challenge
The difficulties of life
And how to cherish the joys.
It will be worth all the variable mixture
For we shall learn it and do it with Him.

I Somehow Always Know

Lord
I love to watch my husband
As he sits before an open hearth—
His eyes following the rhythmic flames
As they circle the massive logs.
Always his index finger
Is pressed against his cheek
And when I interrupt his thoughts
With just a word or two
I somehow always know
I've caught him
In the middle of a prayer.

Consolation

He is old.
His hair is silver-white.
Day after day
For eight dreary months
He walked from his home
To the hospital six blocks away.
Day after day
He sat by her bedside
Gently stroking her feeble hand.
Only occasionally did she recognize him
Or know he was there.
But when she responded
With just a trace of a smile
Tears of elation filled his shadowed eyes.

A week ago Tuesday
He walked to the hospital
For the last time.
Had she lived but one more week
They would have observed
Their sixtieth wedding anniversary.

Until You take him, Lord
May his own consoling words
Be his great sustaining force:
"We've had longer together
Than we'll ever have apart."

Suddenly We Knew

Suddenly we knew
We'd never be the same again. . . .
Tonight we knelt by the side of our bed
Bruised, broken, bewildered
Hearts aching
Tears streaming
Torrents of fear
Saturating our very souls
Lost, lonely, imprisoned
Stricken with regret. . . .
Please hear us, dear God!
Are You there?
Do You see?
Do You care?
Show us, shake us, remake us.

Then out of the desolate darkness
The clear witness of Your voice:
"Behold, I make all things new."
Surrender . . . solace . . . joy.
Unspeakable joy!
O dear God, thank You!
Suddenly we knew
We'd never be the same again.

Totally ... Exclusively

There are thousands of men in the world!
Men come in assorted shapes and sizes—
Tall and short, big and small, wide and lean.
But my husband isn't just any man—
He's *my* man, totally ... exclusively.

I know the sound of his quick step
The shrug of his shoulders
The way he leaves his coffee mug on the floor
When he slumps in his comfortable chair.

I know the way he tosses his pillow
To the foot of the bed
After he kisses me good-night.
I know the cheerful sound of his whistle
The sweet scent of his shaving lotion
The comical, awkward way he helps make
   our bed.

I know how he scowls when he's hungry
How he loves breaded pork chops
How he sprinkles sugar on his tomatoes
And salt on his grapefruit.

I know how failure taunts him
How life challenges him
How he kneels when he prays.

I know his restlessness before a vacation
How he says, "Someday we'll go to
   Switzerland."
(Who knows? Maybe someday we will.)

My husband isn't just any man—
He's *my* man, totally . . . exclusively.
No one will ever know him or love him as
    I do.
We are God's gift to each other.

It Isn't Always Spring

It's going to happen one day—
Maybe on the tenth of April
Maybe on the twelfth of October
Maybe somewhere in between.
But some weary evening after the
   honeymoon
You'll flop down in your favorite chair
Kick off your shoes
And all of a sudden it will hit you:
The sky isn't etched with banners of gold
You're not catching your breath
Between kisses all the time
Butterflies seem to take naps
In marriage it isn't always spring!

In some very pertinent ways
Marriage is indeed a risk.
Our coping abilities are severely tested
Pressures are bigger than any
We've ever encountered.
Often we have to keep giving and giving
Until something breaks
Then we have to keep giving
Until something heals.
In puzzling moments we may have to say
"Here we are, God, your little kids
Help us to grow up."
And then we have to grow up.

God will begin to show us ourselves
In countless new ways.
His love transforms and recreates
He can handle all of our conflicts
All He needs is our willingness to let Him.

Your Glory, Lord

Lord, yesterday was so exciting!
You arranged for me to stand
Before a group of eighty-five women
And share the joy of knowing You.
I talked for thirty minutes.
How responsive the women were—
How attentively they listened.
I trust You were glorified, dear Lord!

Today, I'll be at home
Involved in a myriad of menial tasks:
Sewing buttons on my husband's shirts
Changing the sheets, folding laundry
Cleaning the refrigerator
Shelling walnuts for tomorrow's cookies.
Nobody will pay the slightest attention—
I'll be alone most of the time.
I trust You'll be glorified, dear Lord!

The Choice

"How do you stand it?"
She wanted to know.
"Don't you feel terribly confined?
If I couldn't go to my office
And do something challenging
I think I'd lose my mind!"

O God
Every day of my life I'm challenged
Right here in our comfortable home.
In fact, Lord
There is never sufficient time
To do everything I want to do!
I remember what it's like
To work in an office
To meet the public
To "extend my personality."
But one golden spring morning
There suddenly came an urgent desire
To reacquaint myself
With my own home
My family, my neighbors
My list of "someday" things.
Challenging? Creative?

O Lord, never more so!
With all our loud shouting
For the cause of liberation
I'm thankful that freedom includes
The choice *not* to work
If this is a woman's preference.

Power Status

Lord, thank You
That I am not confused.
I do not constantly question
Who or what I am.
It is tremendously rewarding
Simply to believe
That my power as a woman
Is in *being* a woman!

Until Then

Lord, I really want to be a good wife!
I don't mean "goody-goody."
But rather a wife who believes
With every ounce of her being
That the very foundation
Of good adjustment
Is a growing dedication to You!
I want to be able to say
I like myself as a person
I like my reactions
I like my response to my husband
I like knowing he trusts me.
Help me to accept my husband
Exactly as he is
Even while we anticipate
Your creative changes in us both.
May we follow through
On our unswerving determination
Never to give up on our marriage
Until the precise moment
When YOU give up on us.

Prayer for My Husband

Lord
I am impressed with Paul's statement
Regarding a Christian brother.
He said, "Then there is Apelles
A good man whom the Lord approves."

God, as these words lodge in my heart
They become my personal prayer
For him with whom I share my life.
In his challenging but strenuous work
In the arena of stress and strain
Please encourage and uphold him.
In moments of weakness
May he cry out for Your strength.
May antagonism give way to joy.
May he manifest sterling qualities
In the very thick of the battle.

Lord, I commit myself to this daily prayer
For the husband I have loved so totally
For so many beautiful years.
Continue to make him
A good man whom the Lord approves.

Sunday Morning

We sit in church together
Clasping hands so unobtrusively
That nobody else is aware.
We stand to sing the Doxology
And our fingers touch.
As we reverently bow our heads
In sacred, silent prayer
We both know we are thanking God
For a thousand precious gifts—
Including the gift of our love.
We give our tithes and offerings
With abundant gratitude.
We listen to an anthem of exaltation
And our hearts throb.
We are deeply challenged
By the message of the morning.
With renewed dedication we pray
Lord, may we live what we have heard.
We rise for the benediction
And there is between us
A rare and precious closeness.
We greet the guests and members
To our right and to our left.
Their warm response rekindles love.
We leave the sanctuary together—
Husband and wife.
God, thank You for a meaningful hour
Of joyful worship and praise.

Future Mates

Right now, dear Lord
Somewhere in this giant world
There is a young boy
For whom You have
A unique and special plan.
He may be pulling a wagon
Or fishing by a stream
Or stuffing cookies into his pocket.
His eyes are blue or gray or brown
His hair—is it light or dark?
It doesn't really matter.
It only matters that You hold him close
As he learns to walk with You.
As he grows to be Your man
Give him wisdom from above.
Give him singleness of mind
And purity of heart.
May he set worthy goals
And dream big dreams.
Wherever he is, Lord
Keep him strong and safe
Until in Your own good time
In Your own incredible way
You bring them together
To love, honor, and cherish—
The precious newborn daughter
Who lives next door to us
And the boy who is known to You.

Living Realistically

Lord, teach us both to live realistically
To face life with gut-level honesty.
With so much reading
And so many marriage seminars
We're inclined to conclude
That a slammed door or an hour of sulking
Is final proof of our inability to cope.

God, give us the levelheadedness to accept
Failure, irritations, even anguish
As part and parcel of our spiritual growth.
Help us to recognize
That disagreements and differences
Are included in our family heritage.

Remind us often
That no couple has it all together
Every hour of every day
That contentment is a blessing
Not a signed contract
That emptying the trash or cleaning an oven
Creates more friction than fun
That a cold shower minus a song
Doesn't always indicate regression.
At least once in a while, dear Lord
We ought to be able to give vent to our
    moods
Without one of us suggesting personal
    counseling.

Too often we cling to our storybook dream
Of living happily ever after.

It *will* come true, Lord
But only in the Home You're preparing
    for us.
Until then, give us the maturity to accept
And the willingness to wait.

God of Promises

Lord, this very day
This very hour
My husband and I
Have come face-to-face
With a wrenching crisis.
Our work has folded
Our finances are depleted
Our ambitious plans have exploded
Our glistening dreams are smashed.
We don't know where to turn—
Or scarcely how to pray.
Yet Your Word tells us
There is not a single catastrophe
No matter how staggering
No matter how shattering
That we may not bring to You.
It isn't only that we *may*—
You tell us that we *must*.

Dear God of Promises
You are never lost in our mysteries.
Our eyes are turned toward You.
Keep us from looking back.
While we wait with bleeding hearts
Remind us again, and yet again
That our absence of happiness
Does not mean the absence of God.

A Very Sacred Pledge

Loving each other as we do . . .
    We joyfully acknowledge our sexuality
    As God's priceless gift—
    His unique and exquisite plan
    For our mutual fulfillment.

Loving each other as we do . . .
    We will permit God to use our conflicts
    As lessons in quiet growth.
    We will each focus on the other as a person
    Not as a pleasure or a gimmick.

Loving each other as we do . . .
    We will share the humdrums
    As well as the highlights
    The defeats
    As well as the victories.

Loving each other as we do . . .
    We will not insist on perfection—
    Rather we will anticipate growth.
    We will not compete for the
    mountaintop—
    Rather we'll climb the mountain together.

Loving each other as we do . . .
    We will lift our hearts
    In a celebration of gratitude
    For God's marvelous love
    Which makes our love possible.

Loving each other as we do.

The Dilemma

Lord, I think I'm due
For a good old-fashioned cry.
I can feel it coming on
But I'm in a dilemma.
How shall I handle it, Lord?
Shall I cry it out now
While I'm here by myself
Or shall I wait until
My husband comes home
And use his broad shoulder?
Maybe I'd better cry now
And get it out of my system.
Then when he sees my red, puffy eyes
I'll at least have the aftermath
Of his calming comfort
And dinner won't be quite so late.

Rare Occasions

Lord, help me
To listen patiently
On those rare occasions
When my husband
Takes me in his arms
And tells me
How wonderful he is.

Unexpected Reply

Lord, dear Lord
I'm desperately pleading with You.
Please, please speak to my husband.
You see, he's made a determined decision
And I'm convinced he's totally wrong.
Change his mind, Lord.
Nudge him, prick him
Turn him around, anything—
But capture his attention
And show him I'm right.

Foolish child, don't ask Me
To make your husband
What you want him to be.
Just ask Me to make him
What I want him to be.

Oh, Lord . . .
Then You must work on me.

Prayer for a Husband

Lord, on this first day of the new year
I pray for my husband—
Your dearest love-gift to me.
May he enjoy vibrant health
And a sense of deep satisfaction
In the work You've chosen for him.
Enlarge his vision.
Give him full knowledge of Your will.
Keep him calm and objective
In every difficult situation.
Fulfill his high expectations, Lord.
Encourage and uphold him.
Above all, give him, I pray
A very personal relationship with You.
I claim for him Your promise to Abraham:
"I will bless you
And you shall be a blessing."
Lord, what more could I ask
For the husband who is more than life to me?

Growing in
Difficult Times

Very First Quarrel

I wonder . . . do you remember
Our very first quarrel?
We were sitting at the table
Before a dinner of leftovers.
Teasingly, you took the first bite
Without expressing thanks.
When I asked why, you said
"Honey, it's all been blessed before."

The Calendar

God, there are some years
We would like to cross off the calendar.
This is one of those years.
From January to December my husband and I
Have felt like wounded soldiers
Fighting a losing battle.
Hospitals, life-threatening illness
Surgeries, financial drain, pain
A family death, grief, anxiety
Night-tossing, weariness, silent tears.
Other things, too:
A flooded patio, pieces of roofing
Scattered by howling winds
Two car accidents in bumper-to-bumper
   traffic
Dwindling hope, thundering doubts
The fear-stabbing question
"Lord, don't You love us anymore?"

And yet, dear God
How dare we deny Your day-by-day comfort
At times when we needed it most.
Phone calls bringing encouragement
Notes in the mail
Delicious meals lovingly prepared by friends
A paragraph in a book renewing our trust
Your Word bringing light in the darkness
A sparrow's song during drizzling rain

Your whispered words to our hearts:
"When the pain stays, I stay, too."

O God, You have been our high tower
You have been our hiding place
You have been our sure defense.
The hymn of the psalmist is our hymn, too:
"I will bless the holy Name of God
And not forget the glorious things
    He does."
Over this year's calendar we will finally write
"Surely the Lord was in this place
Though we knew it not."

A Fact

There is no hurt
Worth clinging to
When I love you
As I do!

Please Hurry Home!

Today I awoke
Wanting so much
Just to be alone.
No intrusions
No interruptions
No conversations
Just me and my thoughts.
Then I remembered
In the silence of our house
That this was the day
You left at dawn
For an all-day meeting
Out of town
And suddenly
Knowing I was really alone
I felt terribly lonely.
(Please hurry home!)

Futile Attempt

They are beginning the second year
Of their tempestuous marriage.
"We are miserable," they confessed
"And yet we really love each other."
Lord, help them to see
That their problem
Is not lack of love for each other
But lack of surrender to You.
They are demanding from each other
The infinite satisfaction
That You alone can give.
Dear God, somehow show them
That their marriage
Is in serious trouble
As long as they attempt
To be God to each other.

High Cost of Living

Oh, how I ache for them, Lord
As they walk their separate ways
And yet continue to maintain
The same address.
What a lot of rent to pay
For a house so seldom lived in.
And what a lot of grief to endure
For a marriage so seldom worked at.

He Said–She Said

Another marriage is shattered, Lord.
The divorce will be final next week.

He said it was the breakdown of
   communication
And the subtle infiltration of boredom.
She said it was an accumulation of things.
He said she was unnecessarily preoccupied
With home and children and activities.
She said he stifled her dreams
And ignored her achievements.
He said he felt imprisoned, restricted—
That night after night he got the old
   push-away.
She said he was harsh and brutal
And he often embarrassed her in public.
He said her critical attitudes
Contributed to his sense of inadequacy.
She said she felt lonely and unappreciated
With no claim to personal identity.
He said she wallowed in self-pity
And refused to acknowledge her benefits.
She said he was thriftless and irresponsible.
He said she didn't understand.
She said he didn't care.

Lord, how tragic.
Through all the wearisome years
Neither of them asked what *You* said.

Prayer Request

Lord, perhaps I'm worrying too much
About my devoted friend
Who is so deeply spiritual.
She never misses a church service
Morning or night—
Even though on occasions
Her husband has begged her
To spend a weekend with him.
Every week she attends three study groups
And whenever there is a women's retreat
She's the first to register.
She reads avidly, Lord
Always earmarking pages
To read aloud to her husband.
When she leaves the house
With her Bible and notebook
He settles down with his own problems.
There is never time to voice them.

Lord, her prayer requests
Invariably include her husband:
"Please pray for him.
Our interests are so divergent
And I long for him to change."
Of course, her friends are praying.
And I am praying, too.
But do You mind, Lord
If I pray mostly for my *friend* to change?

The Quarrel

Oh, Lord
It was a foolish quarrel.
Hasty words
Guarded glances
Phantoms of anger and self-pity.

I was wrong
He was wrong
We each knew.

Still our clashing wills
Thrust a wall against the sky
Tall and obstinate—
As immovable as our stubborn pride.
Then all at once
His words came spilling
Like cool spring water
Over jagged rocks:
"Love like ours
Is much too big for this.
Forgive me . . .
Please forgive me."
Sheltered in his arms
I remembered, Lord—

As faith can move a mountain
So love removes a wall.

Cancelled Out

I keep thinking about the man
Who sat behind me in church today.
After every prayer
After the choir anthem
And at least a dozen times
During the sermon
He shouted a boisterous *Amen.*
Then after the service
He shouted at his wife
As they walked toward their car
And, Lord, that angry shout
Cancelled all his *Amens.*

The Gift of Forgiveness

She is a precious woman—
The mother of three children.
She sat in our living room
Longing to pour out her heart.
Finally between sobs
The story unfolded.
She is in counseling now
And she hopes it is helping
But for so long, so endlessly long
She has pushed things back:
Childhood abuse. Love-hate attitudes.
Bitterness. Deep resentments.
Things are not going well
For her husband or her children.
There is so much to forgive—so much.
Then finally the familiar question:
Is it possible to forgive?
Is it really possible?

O God
Speak to her longing heart.
Work Your own wonderful transformation
Within her total being.
Give her the *gift* of forgiveness
Then empower her to forgive herself

For she condemns herself so unmercifully.
You alone can perform the miracle.
Release her. Free her
Until she walks out of her dismal prison
Into a field of fresh yellow daisies.

Hold Us Close

Lord
We're so weary tonight
My husband and I.
Please rest us!
We're thirsty.
Give us Living Water!
We've fallen flat
On our faces.
Pick us up!
We're tired of trying
To maintain the "image."
Let us see You!
Right now
We'd like very much to give up.
Hold us very close!

I Will Wait for You

Right now, my love
I would like to know
What you are thinking
What you are feeling.
This very moment
I know you are hurting deeply.
Your eyes always give you away.
But if for one reason
Or many reasons
You cannot tell me now
If words don't come easily
If somehow you are reluctant
To unlock the door of your heart
Please know I am with you
Just the same.
I will wait for you
With patience and understanding
Because I love you
With all there is of me.

Remind Them Gently

O Lord
Please talk to them—
This beautiful couple
Whose marriage is disintegrating.
God, they've known so much of beauty.
They've endured so much of pain.
They've laughed together, wept together.
They've groped through appalling darkness
Upholding each other step by step.
They've suffered together, triumphed
   together.
They've planned and prayed together.
Now, dear God
Before it is too late
Remind them tenderly of Your command:
"What God has joined together
Let no man put asunder."
Before it is too late
Remind them gently, Lord
That two lives so intricately woven
Into a blended pattern
Can never be wholly separate lives again.

Little Black Bugs

Today I saw two of them—
Little black bugs
With hard, shiny shells.
The tough shells guarded them
From my newspaper attack.

Lord, sometimes I think
My husband and I
Need shells like that
When we are attacking each other.
Or do You have a better way?

Promise Kept

Lord
Years ago on our wedding day
We promised never to say good-night
With anger still hovering—
Never to turn our backs
Hurling bitter words.
But, Lord, must *I* always be the one to yield?
Are personal opinions out for me?
Am I some kind of mechanical robot
Simply because I bear the title "wife"?

I'm sorry, Lord . . .
We both know I'm handcuffed with self-pity
Because I lost last night's argument.
In spite of moments of wrangling
Moments of competitive rivalry
Thank You again for a marriage
Consistently fulfilling
Year after beautiful year.
Teach us both
To express without exploding
To persuade without pouting
To disagree without being disagreeable.

And may we sleep well.

Gift Exchange

She is so lonely
So at loose ends with herself
A sorry picture of dejection.
I had hoped to encourage her when I said
"To some God gives the gift of marriage
To others the gift of *not* being married."
She pushed back a strand of blonde hair
And asked ruefully
"Have you ever been given a gift
That you wanted to exchange?"
I didn't quite know how to answer her.
Lord, what should I have said?

Confession

Lord
It suddenly occurs to me
That the most severe conflicts
In our marriage
Seem to come when I insist
On exposing my husband's faults
Instead of confessing my own.

Try to Remember

Somehow, dear love
I can't seem to dismiss it
From my thoughts.
We argued
And I honestly couldn't help it—
I cried.
You said nothing
And I began to sense
A trace of impatience.
Please, please try to remember
I cry some tears for you
When you can't cry.

Miracle of Healing

O God
Since her husband left her
Over a year ago
Without a word of warning
Without a note of explanation
Her heart is so shattered
Her defeat is so great.

How I wish I could capture a sunbeam
And wrap it carefully in a small box
So that anytime she wanted to
She could reach in and pull out
At least a sliver of sunlight.

If only I could build her a cabin
Under a blue, blue sky
A place all her very own
A place of serenity
Where she could quietly rest
And regain peace and composure.

I know my wistful dreams
Are far, far beyond
Any accomplishment of mine
So I'll simply continue to do
What I have been doing day by day:
I'll pray and trust . . .
Pray and trust . . .
Until that incredible day
When You will perform
A miracle of healing

So amazing, so complete
That she will proclaim with joy
"He has turned my darkness
Into dazzling light!"

Financial Status

Please, Lord
Rid us of all brooding thoughts
About our finances.
Make us channels of giving
Rather than champions in getting.
May we never lose sight of the fact
That all that we have is Yours.
Keep us poised and positive
And genuinely grateful.
Release us from the compulsive urge
To compete, to surpass, to overextend.
Make us wary of "pay later" expenditures.
Give us the good common sense
To see that there is no way
To keep our heads and hearts together
If money is pulling us apart.

Lord
We believe it is according to wisdom
To budget regularly
To save consistently
To discuss sufficiently
To give lavishly.
May we keep each other updated
Regarding our financial status.
Impress on us this spiritual challenge:
"The real measure of our wealth
Is how much we'd be worth
If we lost all our money."

Above all, dear Lord
Make it our deep, settled conviction
That our financial accumulation
Is never our primary protection.
You are!

The Challenge

It may be true, dear God
That my husband and I had more to live on
A year ago than we have today
But it is equally true
That we have just as much to live *for*.
The real values of our lives remain
Solid, stable, unshifting.
Our financial loss has in no way
Diminished the value of a single friendship.
We have lost nothing of human dignity
And we are discovering spiritual realities
Full of wonder and sheer delight.
Our faith in Your loving-kindness
Adds growing serenity to our guided lives.
You are making us increasingly aware
That what we *are* is vastly more vital
Than our fondest possessions.
Above all, You are teaching us
That a limited salary is our shining
　challenge
To trust and exalt our limitless God!

For Better, For Worse

Lord, over forty years ago
We made a solemn promise:
"For better or for worse."
Today we are stumbling through "worse."
Though our emotions are a bewildered
   mixture
Of agony and love, please quiet us, Lord.
Free us from the desire to retaliate.
Above all, help us both to remember
We are as bound to our promise today
As we were yesterday
When we basked in the sunlight of "better."
Even now, dear Lord
Help us to make it better again
By not putting off what we both know
We must eventually do
If healing is to take place.
The simple but beautiful word is *forgiveness*.

Help Them Just Now

I keep thinking of them, Lord
Thinking and thinking. . . .

Sitting in the booth next to theirs
I heard but fragments
Of their troubled conversation.
She reproached him
For his thoughtlessness
His shameful unconcern.
With hatred in his voice
He whirled his bitter accusations—
Then he grabbed the check
And left her sitting there alone.
I wonder—is she still alone
This cold and rainy night?

Forgive me, Lord
Please forgive me. . . .

Too often I take for granted
The days
The nights
The gentle moments in between
When my husband holds me close
And softly whispers:
"God was good to give me you."

Squabbles

"Why do you always—"
"Hey, wait a minute—
I don't always . . ."
"You interrupted me.
How do you know
What I was going to say?"
"I don't know
But whatever it was
I don't *always*."

"See, you *never* listen."
"Yes, I do!"
"When?"
"When you call dinner."

O dear Lord
The Creator of our lives
And of our marriage
Thank You for the spontaneous laughter
That so often resolves
Our stupid, childish squabbles.

Words

I saw her drooping shoulders
Her sad, misty eyes
As his bitter words of sarcasm
Blew across her animation
And choked the story
She longed so much to share. . . .

Words!
O dear God
Words can be so devastating
So destructive.
They shock and numb
They sting and torment.
In three brief minutes
They can disfigure a soul.
They permeate the air
Like a suffocating poison.
Lord, Your own Word convicts us:
"So also the tongue is a small thing
But what enormous damage it can do."
Teach us to cope tactfully
Even in moments of disagreement.
Make us carefully selective
And lovingly protective
In the creative use of words.

Poignant Hurt

Laughing raucously
He said to his chagrined wife
"I wouldn't eat that
If I were you, Fatty!"
All eyes turned toward her
And when I saw her poignant hurt
I wasn't at all surprised
That she weighed two hundred pounds.
What else did she have?

Loving through Obedience
and Responsibility

Lessons in Patience

Dear Lord
After forty-three years of marriage
I think perhaps I've learned
A few practical lessons in patience.
For example, it isn't always easy
To laugh at my own jokes—
Especially when we have dinner guests
And my husband tells *my* jokes.

The Crown

God, through the years
Of our married life
You have been holding a crown
About ten feet above my husband's head.
He was simply too busy
Loving and serving to notice.
But I saw it.
Not only did I see it—
I watched him grow into it.

Fresh Insight

We were shopping for new shoes
For her eight-year-old
A week or two ago.
After our shopping spree
The three of us
Stopped for a dish of ice cream.
During our pleasant conversation
We talked a lot about how the years
Change our concepts about marriage.
I loved what she said:

"You know, when we were first married
I felt very confident
That our love would steady our marriage.
But after almost fifteen years
I am convinced
That our marriage strengthens our love."
Lord, I was personally challenged
By her fresh insight.
It spoke to me!

High Pedestal

Lord, forgive me
For the times
I put myself
On a pedestal so high
That my husband
Can't reach me.
So often it is
When he needs me most.

Bargain-Basement Marriage

Several weeks ago
I heard a short but pointed conversation
Between two male executives:
"Well, George, it really paid off last night.
I must have done everything right."
"Great, Jim! Was it worth
The new ring you bought her?"
"Sure thing." *(Pensive pause.)*
"I wonder what it will take next time?
Some marriage we've got!" *(Raucous
    laughter.)*

A cunning, conniving wife
Or a manipulating husband
Had made a bargain:
Sex in exchange for a diamond ring.
Result: A bargain-basement marriage.
This is subtle, sad, sick.
This is a bribe. This is destructive.
Sexuality, shabbily treated
Reaps a marriage basically cheated.

The Gift

Lord, it happened so unexpectedly:
I had just finished
Vacuuming the bedroom carpet
When there came an overwhelming urge
To pray for my husband.
At first I pushed it aside
But the thought was relentless.
It came with increasing urgency:
"Pray for your husband."

I obeyed.
Kneeling by the blue couch
In our quiet living room
I surrendered my husband to You.
I asked You to sustain him
To diminish his problems
To focus his attention on You.
When I glanced at my watch
It was ten minutes after four.

Later, at the dinner table
My husband quietly said
"All day long I struggled
With insuperable problems.
Then suddenly, unaccountably
A little after four o'clock
God saturated me with peace
And I accomplished more in an hour
Than in all the preceding hours."

O dear God
Thank You for teaching me
An invaluable lesson:
I can give my husband
No greater gift
Than the gift of a praying heart.

Still More

I love you!
You are so uncluttered
So open to love and laughter and life.
There are no dark, musty corners in you
No cobwebbed crevices
Of hatred and hostility.
There are no rusty nails of bitterness
No dusty cabinets of prejudice and pretense.

I love you!
You weave within me a delicate pattern
Of wind and sea
Of sunlight and stars.
You soothe me, comfort me, release me.
You are like a quiet song.

I love you!
You are so willingly, so totally
Surrendered to God.
I know Him better because of you.

I love you!
When I awaken in the morning
I shall love you still more.

As God Intended It

Sex as God intended it
 Is rich and refreshing
 It is longing and belonging
 It is trustful mutuality
 It is the cooperative experience
 Of meeting each other's stirring needs.

Sex as God intended it
 Can be timid yet daring
 Awkward yet bewitching
 Quiet yet explosive.
 At times it races up a windswept hill
 At other times it is as quiet as dawn.

Sex as God intended it
 Is a language all its own
 It is more than a moment of passion
 It is a promise of fidelity
 It is more than a passing episode
 It is a source of life
 It is venturous rather than violent
 It delights rather than defrauds.

Sex as God intended it
 Is a glorious celebration
 Of "the wonder of us"
 The wonder of God!
 It is a dynamic gift
 To be reverently treasured
 And joyfully cherished.

Breakfast Prayer

Lord, I'll never forget
My husband's prayer one morning
At the breakfast table.
"Please, Lord, make me the husband
You want me to be—
First for Your sake
Then for her sake."

We were having waffles
That morning.
As I poured the syrup
I felt my heart pouring out, too.
I knew I could trust a husband
Who prayed like that.

Healthy Change?

Lord, I can't help but wonder—
Isn't there anything else
In the whole wide world
To write about, think about
Talk about, read about
But the sex explosion
Which has become so all-absorbing?
So many books on sex . . .
So many television talk shows . . .
So many sermons, seminars
And sex education classes.
It's an alluring subject, Lord—
Stimulating, fascinating
And beautiful, too.
With gratitude I recognize sex
As a marvelous part
Of Your creative plan
But You have other plans, too!
Would it please You—
And would the change be healthy—
If we'd give an equal amount of
Space, time, print, discussion
To a prayer explosion
Or a tithing explosion
Or a love-thy-neighbor explosion
For at least a year or two?
I may stand alone in thinking so
But I do think so!

Discovery

This we have discovered—
This is always true:
There's
nothing
we
can't
love
each
other
through.

A Serious Thing

It is a serious thing
To make a commitment to somebody else
Even when the love is real.
It puts enormous demands on us
It tests our patience and integrity.
Marriage deals with real problems
As does all of life.
But what makes it so stupendous is this:
The One who hears our commitment to each
   other
Is eternally committed to us.

A Man of Talents

Lord, You've blessed my husband
With an amazing amount of talent.
He can do so many things well.
I love to listen to his deep, rich voice
When he sings a solo.
I love to watch him direct a huge choir.
I love the way he paints commercial signs.
When he leads a Bible study
I am always amazed at his fresh insights.
He makes our yard look like a beautiful
   park.
However, I've made one interesting
   discovery:
With a few tools in his hand
In no time at all
The dripping faucet in our kitchen
Becomes a rushing stream.

A Better Way

My love . . . I remember
The day I said to you
So defensively, so decisively
"That's just my way of doing things.
You'll have to get used to me!"
After you left for your office
God said to me
So pointedly, so pertinently
"Why don't you settle
For MY way of doing things?
You'll be much more fun to live with!"

With All My Heart

I want to assure you, my husband
It is my honest intent
To uphold and support you always.
My emotions, like yours, will fluctuate.
There will be painful times
Frustrating and puzzling times
But I will not renege.
I may not always be able to give you
Total, unconditional love.
Only God can do that.
But it is the goal toward which
I will faithfully strive.
I am committed to stand with you
As God brings to joyful fruition
His plan for our lives.

What do you need today?
Laughter? A time of sharing
Your heart's desires?
Are you discouraged? Anxious?
Do you need my touch?
Do you need some space for a while?
Do you need me to pray for you?

Sometimes I'll be right
Sometimes I'll be wrong.
But the important thing is
That you know without a doubt
That I do what I do
Because I love and cherish you
With all my heart.

Easier by Far

O Lord
Never could I hide my love for him—
The husband who makes my life complete.
It would be easier by far
To hide a million stars
Or quiet the pounding sea
Or stop the rustle of the wind
Or stuff a billowing cloud into my pocket.

Wrong Choice

Just today I read
That one gentle touch
Is worth a thousand words.
Forgive me, dear Lord!
Forgive me, my husband!
Too often I've chosen
The thousand words.

I Wonder

I wonder, dear Lord
Is my husband aware
When I set our small table—
When I serve him veal cutlets
Or chicken-fried steak
Or sometimes an old-fashioned stew
Is he ever aware
(Between sips and bites)
That it's really my heart
I'm serving him?

Submit to Each Other

How I thank You, dear Lord
That the principle of submission
In no way devalues my potential.
I can make decisions without
Always running to my husband.
I am not pushed aside
Like an ornament after Christmas.
My capabilities are not shelved.
I do not feel threatened.
I don't play coy little games
To prove my "submissiveness."
I am a woman with a legitimate right
To my individuality.
I need not stifle my intellect
Or repress my ideas
For fear of deflating
My husband's masculinity.

The shimmering secret is this:
The more totally we submit to You, dear God
The more joyfully we submit to each other.
I believed this the first year
Of our marriage
With a few ominous clouds
Hovering over my independent spirit.
Today I believe it
With unwavering conviction.
It works as Your Word said it would.
"Honor Christ by submitting to each other."

Creative Task

Lord, You are giving me
The stupendous task
Of helping my husband become
All You intend him to be.
It startles me, God.
It overwhelms me.
I am a partner in Your creation!
Help me to love him
With all the love of my being.
Keep refueling me, God
For too often I run low on love.
And, Lord
Help me never to use "I love you"
As a crutch or a cover-up
When I should first say, "I'm sorry."

Marriage

Marriage!
It's rough. It's tough. It's work.
Anybody who says it isn't
Has never been married.
Marriage has far bigger problems
Than toothpaste squeezed
From the middle of the tube.

Marriage means . . .
Grappling, aching, struggling.
It means putting up
With personality weaknesses
Accepting criticism
And giving each other freedom to fail.
It means sharing deep feelings
About fear and rejection.
It means turning self-pity into laughter
And taking a walk to gain control.

Marriage means . . .
Gentleness and joy
Toughness and fortitude
Fairness and forgiveness
And a walloping amount of sacrifice.

Marriage means . . .
Learning when to say nothing
When to keep talking
When to push a little
When to back off.
It means acknowledging

"I can't be God to you—
I need Him, too."

Marriage means . . .
You are the other part of me
I am the other part of you.
We'll work through
With never a thought of walking out.

Marriage means . . .
Two imperfect mates
Building permanently
Giving totally
In partnership with a perfect God.

Marriage, my love, means us!